Fright Night Flight

by Laura Krauss Melmed • illustrated by Henry Cole

SCHOLASTIC INC.

New York   Toronto   London   Auckland   Sydney
Mexico City   New Delhi   Hong Kong   Buenos Aires

For my nephews, Andrew and Jeremy Melmed
—L.K.M.

To Cole "Schtinkers" Burrell, who was the world's best college roommate,

who taught me the difference between a keely and dearie, and who makes

the world a funnier place and a greener place, with love from Henny
—H.C.

ISBN 0-439-57623-7

12 11 10 9 8 7 6 5 4 3   8/0

Printed in the U.S.A.   40

First Scholastic printing, September 2003

Typography by Elynn Cohen

Fright Night Flight

The moon sails high, the wind moans low, the Fright Night Flight is set to go!

With hat and cat, away I zoom
upon my super jet-fueled broom.

First stop, off we pop
on a craggy mountaintop.
Spooky castle, creaky floor—
who is opening the door?

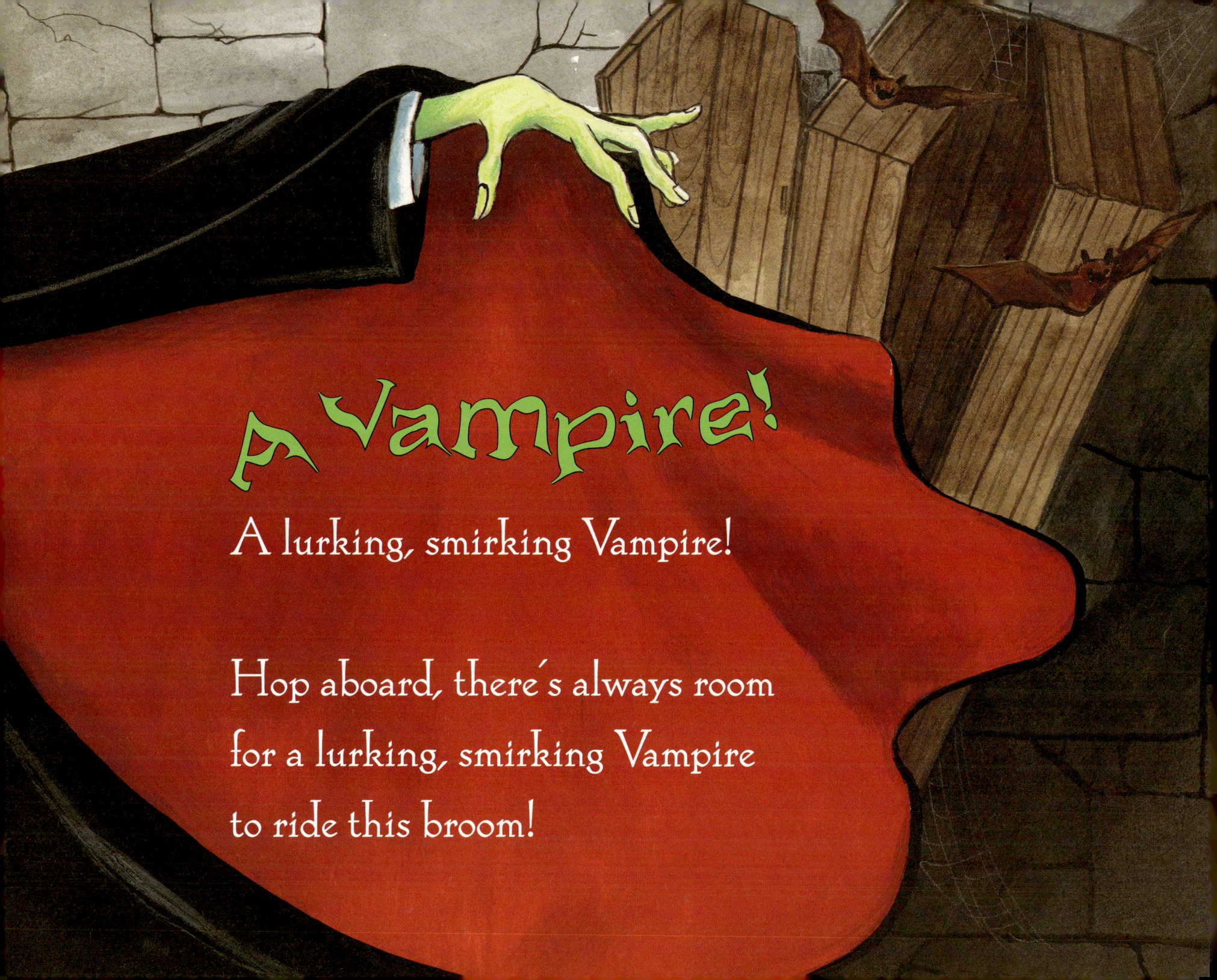

A Vampire!

A lurking, smirking Vampire!

Hop aboard, there's always room
for a lurking, smirking Vampire
to ride this broom!

Second stop—it isn't very
merry in this cemetery.
Who is slouching through the gloom,
crouching down behind each tomb?

A WErEwOlf!

A howling, growling Werewolf!

Hop aboard, there's always room
for a howling, growling Werewolf
and a lurking, smirking Vampire
to ride this broom.

Third stop, House of Dread, owned by folks who once were dead.
Here a howl, there a roar—who's that coming *through* the door?

A GHOST!

A *boo-boo-boo-oo-gity* Ghost!
Hop aboard, there's always room
for a *boo-boo-boo-oo-gity* Ghost,
a howling, growling Werewolf,

and a lurking, smirking Vampire
to ride this broom.

Hospital upon a hill—
don't come here if you are ill!
This is the Mad Doctor's lab.
Who just got up from the slab?

A MONSTER!

A hulking, skulking Monster!

Hop aboard, there's always room
for a hulking, skulking Monster,
a *boo-boo-boo-oo-gity* Ghost,
a howling, growling Werewolf,
and a lurking, smirking Vampire
to ride this broom.

Wait! Wait! We forgot
someBODY at that last spot.
First a rattle, then a bark.

Who's approaching in the dark?

Hop aboard, there's always room
for a jittery, skittery Skeleton,
a hulking, skulking Monster,
a *boo-boo-boo-oo-gity* Ghost,
a howling, growling Werewolf,
and a lurking, smirking Vampire
to ride this broom.

Next stop, the museum.

Didn't I just hear a scream?

Something's strange about this place!

Who is missing from that case?

A Mummy!

A musty, dusty Mummy!

Hop aboard, there's always room
for a musty, dusty Mummy,
a jittery, skittery Skeleton,
a hulking, skulking Monster,
a *boo-boo-boo-oo-gity* Ghost,
a howling, growling Werewolf,
and a lurking, smirking Vampire
to ride this broom.

Attention, ghouls and fiendish friends,
the Fright Night Flight has reached its end!
Prepare for landing! Hold on tight!
We'll touch down by the full moon's light,
and soon we'll be parading through
a neighborhood well known to YOU.

We'll find your house
(we know the street)
and . . . ring . . . your . . . doorbell . . .